Foreword

Who wouldn't enjoy receiving a hand embroidered, personalized gift? What an expression of love!

This book will help you express your own love when you create wedding, baby, birthday or Christmas gifts for the special people in your life.

Beautiful color photographs of embroidered projects will give you the inspiration to create your own monogrammed items. To make this process fool-proof, there are 18 pages of iron-on transfers—alphabets, borders and designs. Just select the monogram or designs you want to use, iron them on and add your stitches. It's as easy as that.

See the stitch instructions on pages 61-64 to refresh your memory or to add to your repertoire of stitches.

Along with the original designs in this book, we've included some vintage designs from our embroidery collection—designs that are reminiscent of the 1930s and 40s. You'll be delighted with these nostalgic reminders of the past.

Take pleasure in sharing your creations with others when you give your embroidered gifts of love.

General Embroidery Instructions

Fabric

Almost any fabric can be embroidered. It's best to use a medium weight fabric with a tight weave. Of course solid fabrics are best, but stripes or subtle prints can also work. Premade items such as napkins, sheets and pillowcases, tea towels, and pillows are excellent items to be stitched.

Threads

Most of the designs in this book were worked using 100% cotton embroidery floss. There are other specialty threads that would work well also, such as pearl cotton, silk, rayon, metallic, or linen threads.

Needles

Remember, the larger the number of the needle, the smaller it is. The needles most commonly used are called embroidery needles. They are very sharp so that they go through the fabric easily. Most of the designs in this book were stitched using a #8 embroidery needle.

Embroidery Hoop

When choosing an embroidery hoop, select one that is larger than the design you will be stitching. The hoop will produce tension on the fabric so that stitches will be uniform and neat and you'll have a nicer finished piece.

Stitches

A variety of stitches have been used in the projects in this book. Please refer to the project instructions as well as the stitch diagrams for best results.

Tips for embroidery

1. Cut floss no more than 18 inches long. Longer pieces tend to flatten, twist, and look a bit worn. Also, longer pieces tend to knot up more often.
2. Use small, sharp scissors to cut out mistakes. You will be less apt to accidentally snip the fabric.
3. Use scraps of fabric to practice new stitches before you stitch on your actual project. Save the pieces and make a patchwork sampler later. You'll have a permanent record of the stitches to refer to.
4. Sign and date your original designs. It will help you keep track of your embroidery progress.

For extra special designs, add beads, buttons and charms to your piece.

Monograms

Monograms can include a single initial or a triple monogram.

For wedding gifts, triple initial monogams include the bride's first, maiden, and married initials. Another choice might include the bride's first initial, husband's first initial and the married surname in the center.

A monogram in which the last initial is in the center and larger than the other two is also popular. One alphabet in this book contains both small and large versions for this purpose (see alphabet on pages 24 & 26). See an example of this type of monogram on the Pink Satin pillowcase, page 6.

Iron-On Transfer Instructions

Transferring Designs to Fabric

All the transfers in this leaflet are designed to be used more than once. The iron's temperature setting, the length of time the iron is on the transfer, and the amount of pressure placed on the iron will affect the transfer. These three factors determine the number of times the design can be clearly transferred. Therefore, if you plan to use a transfer several times, use the least amount of heat and the shortest amount of time possible to transfer the design.

Always prewash fabric before transferring designs; do not use fabric softener.

Small test transfers are included throughout the leaflet. These should be used before beginning your project in order to determine the best iron temperature and length of time needed to get a good transfer. Follow the steps below to use transfers:

1. Preheat iron for five minutes on appropriate setting for fabric being used. Do not use steam.
2. Transfer ink may bleed through fabric; protect ironing board cover by placing a clean piece of fabric or paper under fabric.
3. (Note: the inked transfer is the reverse of what will appear on fabric.) Always test on a similar fabric. Cut out a transfer. Place inked side down, on right side of fabric. Place iron on transfer; hold for five seconds. Do not slide iron. Pick up iron and move to another position on transfer so areas under steam holes are transferred. Carefully lift one corner of transfer to see if design has been transferred to fabric. If not, place iron on transfer a few more seconds.

When satisfied with results of test transfer, cut out desired designs. Pin designs to fabric and transfer in the same manner as test transfer.

If you do not get a satisfactory transfer (the lines did not show up well) or if you are using a dark fabric, there is an alternative method of transferring a design to fabric. Trace design onto tracing paper. Place dressmaker's tracing paper, coated side down, on right side of fabric. Place traced design, right side down, on dressmaker's tracing paper. Use a stylus or a dull pencil to draw over line of design.

If you have ironed a transfer several times and the transfer ink is starting to fade, place a piece of aluminum foil under the fabric. If you wish to use a transfer after the transfer ink is gone, use dressmaker's tracing paper method or draw over lines of design with an iron-on transfer pencil or pen and follow manufacturer's instructions to transfer design onto fabric. Transfer pencils and pens are available at fabric and craft stores.

Table of Contents

Note:

Some of our alphabet transfers are taken from an antique book of ancient alphabets and may not contain the letters x and z. Check them before choosing to be sure they include your initials.

Pillowcases

Lovely Lavender

Embroidery floss	DMC	Coats & Clark
Pink	602	3071

Transfer - page 16

Monogram - pink split stitch, 3 strands

Totally Turquoise

Embroidery floss	DMC	Coats & Clark
Purple	333	4101

Transfer - pages 18 & 20

Monogram - purple satin stitch, 3 strands
purple couching stitch, 1 strand

Hot Pink

Embroidery floss	DMC	Coats & Clark
Green	907	6001
Lavender	340	7110
Light Blue	964	7167

Transfer - page 22

Monograms - green, lavender, and light blue satin stitch, 2 strands

Pillowcases

Dream

Embroidery floss	DMC	Coats and Clark
Blue	828	7167
White		

Transfer - page 16

Stitch using 2 strands

"Dream" - blue satin stitch
Stars - white double cross stitches
Moon - white satin stitch

Pink Satin

Embroidery floss	DMC	Coats and Clark
Green	955	6030
Pink	3354	3087

Transfer - pages 24 & 26

Stitch using 2 strands

Monogram - green satin stitch and back stitch with pink laid work and cross bars

Pastel Green

Embroidery floss	DMC	Coats and Clark
Green	955	6030

Transfer - pages 48 & 50

Stitch using 2 strands

Monogram - Satin stitch and couching stitch

Napkins

Good as Gold

Embroidery floss	DMC	Coats & Clark
Gold	833	2412

Transfer - pages 28 & 30

Stitch using 3 strands

Monogram - gold satin stitch
Outline of monogram - gold split stitch

True Blue

Embroidery floss	DMC	Coats & Clark
Blue	809	7030
Green	522	6017
Pink	3354	3087
Gold	833	2412
Lavender	340	710

Transfer - pages 32 & 44

Stitch using 2 strands

Monogram - blue satin stitch
Vine - green split stitch
Small flowers - pink, gold, lavender single lazy daisy stitch

Royal Purple

Embroidery floss	DMC	Coats & Clark
Lavender	340	7110

Transfer - pages 48 & 50

Stitch using 2 strands

Monogram - lavender stem stitch

In the Pink

Embroidery floss	DMC	Coats & Clark
Medium pink	604	3001
Light pink	3354	3087
Green	522	6017

Transfer - page 38

Stitch using 2 strands

Monogram - pink satin stitch and split stitch
Vines - green split stitch
Leaves - green lazy daisies
Flowers - medium pink bullion knots

Note:

The roses and vines were added to this initial. Lazy daisies could also be used. Try adding vines and flowers to any of the other initials in this manner.

Card Party

Embroidery floss	DMC	Coats & Clark
Red	321	3500
Black		

Transfers - page 42

Stitch using 3 strands

Monograms - black satin stitch with red couching stitch for the center line
Spade, club, diamond - red split stitch

Note:

Transfer the spade, club, diamond (or heart) onto the piece first, then center the letters within the shapes and transfer them.

Table Linens

Scotties (vintage)

Embroidery floss	DMC	Coats & Clark
Red	349	3013
Black		
White		

Transfers - page 20

Stitch using 2 strands

Large scottie - white satin stitch
Small scotties - black satin stitch
Bows, eyes, noses - red satin stitch
Border - black and white couching stitch
Black small squares - black satin stitch

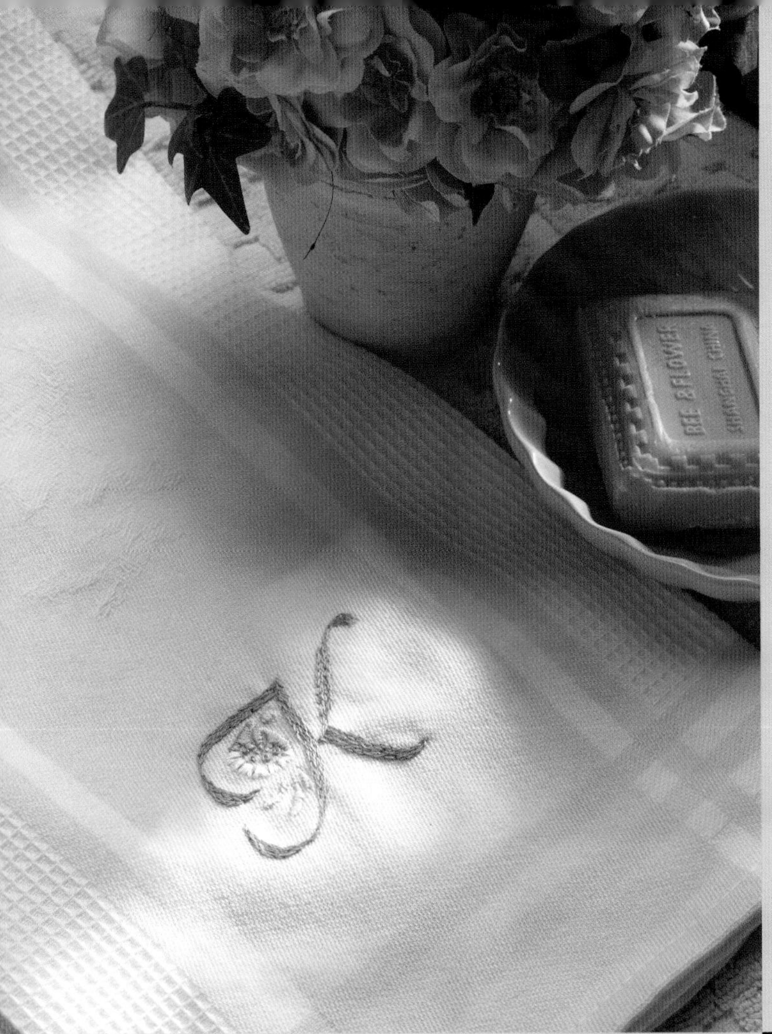

Guest Towels

Pink Parfait

Embroidery floss	DMC	Coats & Clark
Pink	316	3084
Lt Pink	224	3146
Green	504	6016
White		

Transfer - pages 18 & 20 and flower transfer page 32

Stitch using 3 strands

Monogram - pink stem stitch
Flower - lt. pink satin stitch
Bottom edge of flower - white satin stitch with pink straight stitch
Leaves - green satin stitch
Center of flower - pink French knots

Note:

The flower was added to the initial. Any of the other small flower transfers could be used here or on any of the other alphabets.

Shower of Flowers (vintage)

Embroidery floss	DMC	Coats & Clark
Gold	742	2302
Turquoise	519	7005
Navy	796	7100
Green	3345	6318

Transfer - page 30

Stitch using 2 strands

Flowers - navy, turquoise and gold satin stitch and straight stitch
Flower centers - navy satin stitch
Stems - green back stitch
Leaves - green satin stitch

Guest Towel

A Touch of Violet

Embroidery floss	DMC	Coats & Clark
Dk. green	469	6267
Lt. green	581	6256
Purple	3835	4301
Lavender	153	4303
Pink	3354	3087

Transfer - pages 44 & 46

Stitch using 2 strands

Monogram - dk. green satin stitch outlined with split stitch
Detail on monogram - purple satin stitch
Vine - lt. green split stitch
Flowers - pink, purple and lavender lazy daisy and French knot

Table Runner

Green Elegance

Embroidery floss	DMC	Coats & Clark
Blue	828	7159
Lavender	3042	4222
Green	523	6316

Transfer - pages 38 & 40

Stitch using 2 strands

Monogram - blue, lavender and green split stitch

Basket of Flowers (vintage)

Embroidery floss	DMC	Coats & Clark
Pink (basket)	604	3087
Green	988	6239
Gold	742	2302
Blue	825	7023
Peach	353	3868
Grey	415	8390
Lavender	3743	8398
Lt. pink (dot flowers)	818	3173

Transfer - page 42

Stitch using 3 strands

Basket - pink stem stitch and cross stitch
Bow - blue stem stitch
Blue flower - straight stitch
Blue flower center - gold French knots
Peach flower - straight stitch
Peach flower center - lavender French knots
Lt. pink and lavender flowers - French knots
Gold flower - satin stitch
Vines - green stem stitch
Leaves - green lazy daisy

Needle Art (vintage)

Embroidery floss	DMC	Coats & Clark
Green	319	6211
Pink	956	3152
Gold	742	2302
Ivory	712	2275

Transfer - page 40

Stitch using 3 strands

Flowers - pink straight stitch
Flower centers - gold French knots
Design - ivory four sided stitch
Leaves - green lazy daisy
Vines - green stem stitch

Note:

We mounted this vintage embroidered tea towel on a square artist canvas and trimmed it with a green-and-white check ribbon.

ABCDEF
GHIJKLM
NOPQRS
TUVWYZ
Dream

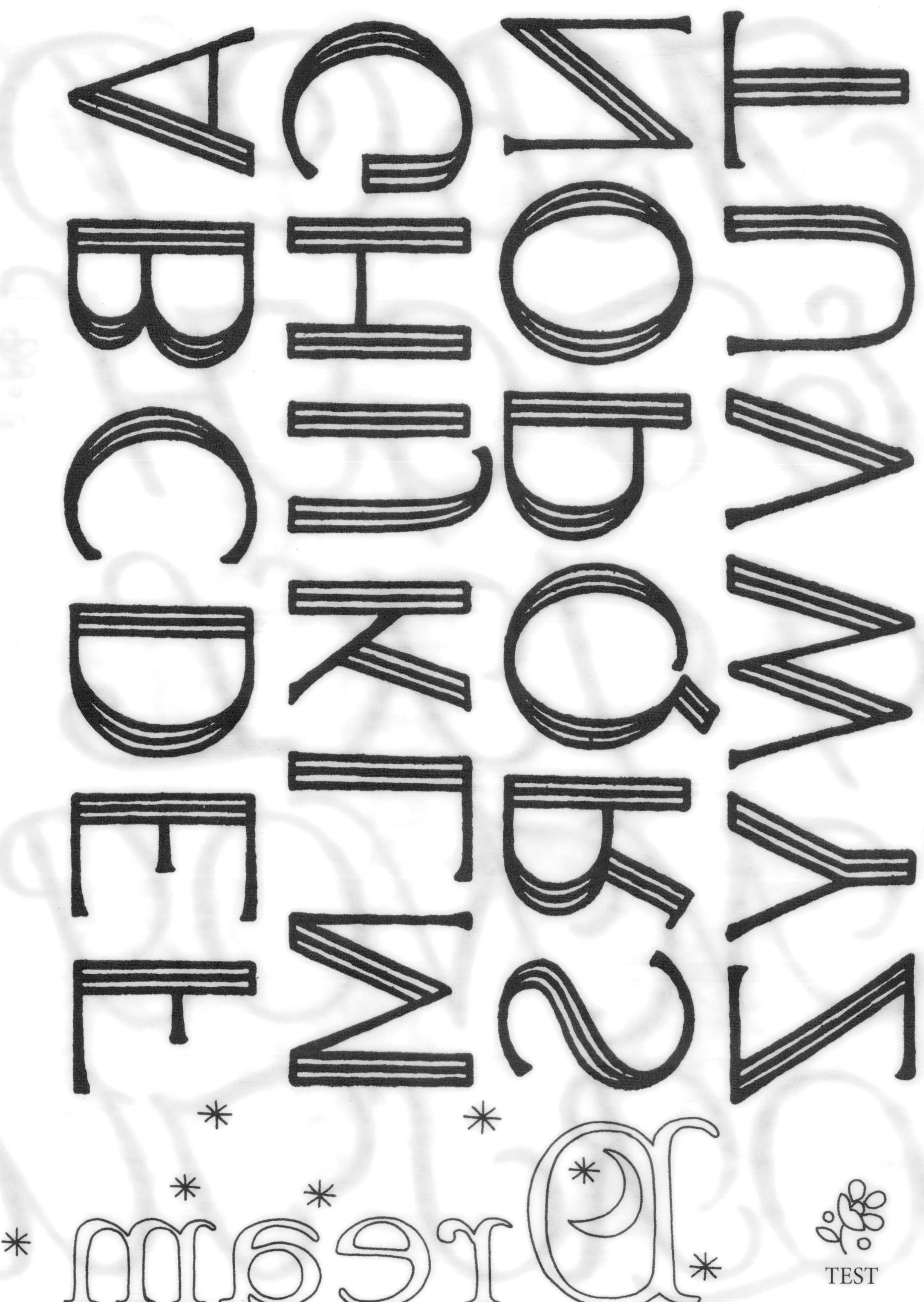
TEST

TEST

TEST

TEST

TEST

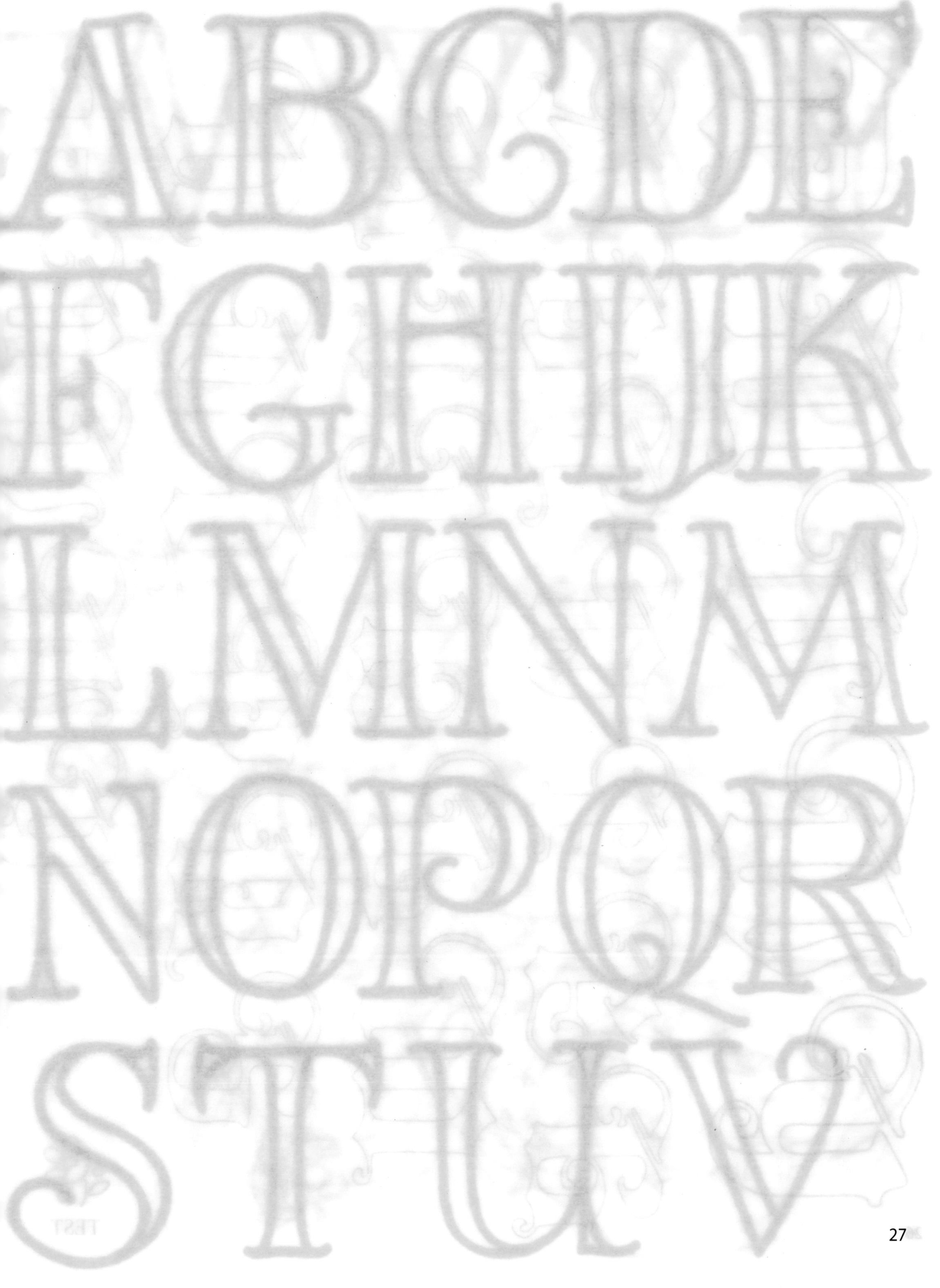

A B C D E

F G H I J K

I L M N M

N O P Q R

S T U V

TEST

TEST

TEST
PRINCESS
Bébé

abcdefghi
jklmnopqr
stuvwxyz

TEST

TEST

ABCDEFGHIJKLM
NOPQRSTUVWXYZ

TEST

TEST

TEST

TEST

A B C D E F
G H I J K L M
N O P Q R S T
U V W X Y Z

TEST

Pajama Game

Embroidery floss	DMC	Coats & Clark
Blue	792	7023
White		

Transfer - page 50

Stitch using 2 strands

Monogram - blue satin stitch and stem stitch
French knots - white

Bébé

Embroidery floss	DMC	Coats & Clark
Lavender	340	7110
Pink	3716	3127
Green	989	6238
Blue	3755	7030

Transfer - page 34

Stitch using 3 strands

Letters - lavender, pink, green, blue split stitch
Accent marks - pink and blue lazy daisy stitch

Niño

Embroidery floss	DMC	Coats & Clark
Green	907	6001
Pink	600	3401
Turquoise	995	7010
Orange	947	2332

Transfer - page 34

Stitch using 3 strands

Letters - green, pink, turquoise and orange stem stitch
Border around neck and arms - green, pink, turquoise and orange stem stitch

Baby Clothes

Emily

Embroidery floss	DMC	Coats & Clark
Pink	605	3127

Transfer - page 30

Letters - pink stem stitch, 3 strands
Center of letters - French knots, 2 strands

Garland of Flowers

Embroidery floss	DMC	Coats & Clark
Green	907	6001
Orange	741	2327
Yellow	3823	2296
Lavender	340	7110
Lt. Blue	747	7053

Transfer - page 30

Stitch using 2 strands

Leaves and vines - green satin stitch and couching stitch
Flowers - alternate with orange, yellow, lavender and blue split stitch
Center of flowers - straight stitch and satin stitch

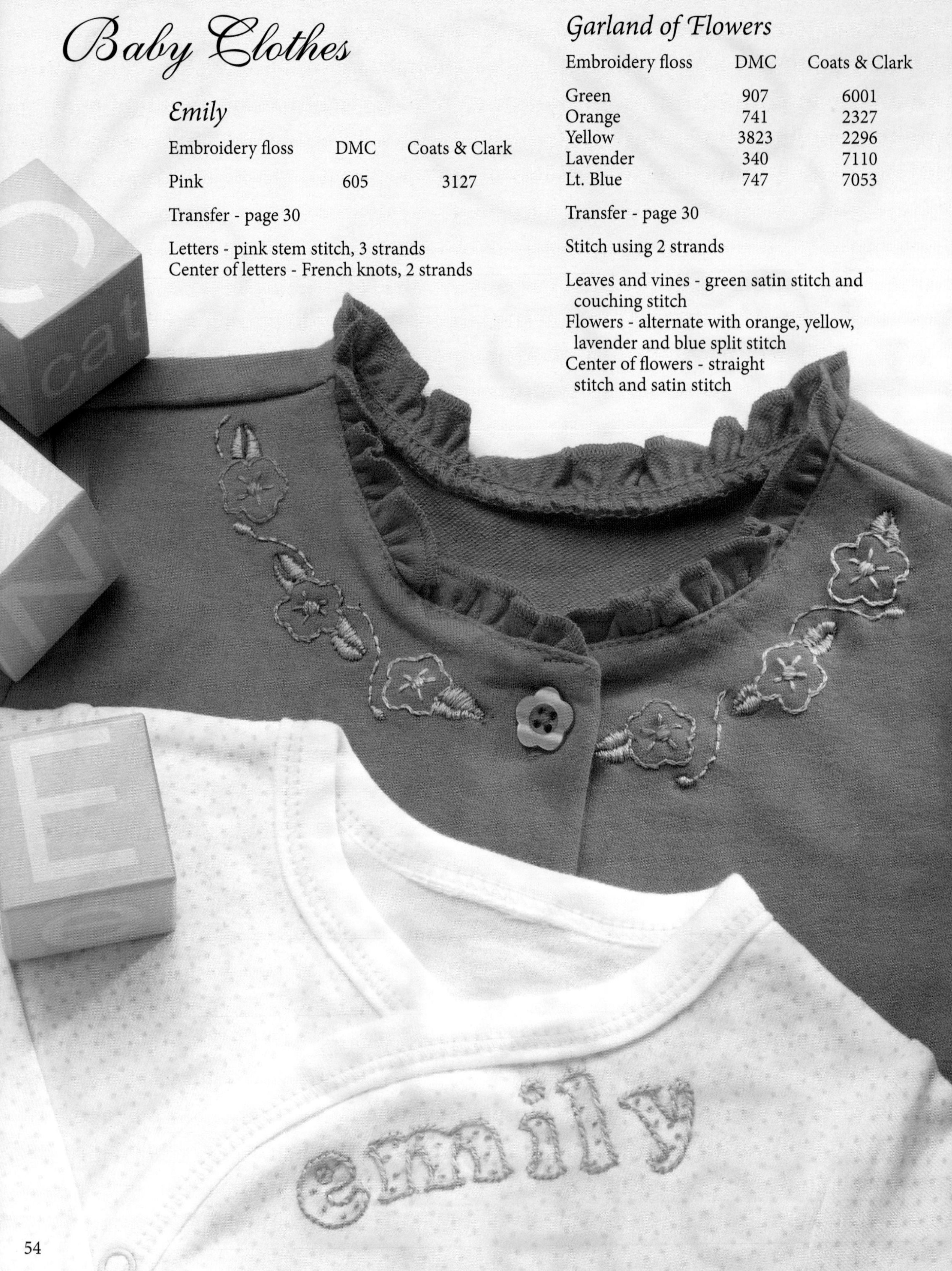

Baby Clothes

Little Star

Embroidery floss	DMC	Coats & Clark
Blue	336	7981
Gold	3820	60 (rayon)

Transfer - page 32

Stitch using 3 strands

Letters - blue satin stitch
Stars - gold double cross stitch

Princess

Embroidery floss	DMC	Coats & Clark
Pink	3716	3127
Blue	340	7110
Gold	3820	60 (rayon)
Red	666	90 (rayon)
Blue	796	85 (rayon)
Green	910	65 (rayon)

Transfer - page 34

Letters - lavender and pink laced running stitch, 3 strands
Crown - gold satin stitch, 3 strands
Points on crown - red, blue and green French knots, 2 strands

Photo Albums

Embroidered Memories (wedding album)

Embroidery floss	DMC	Coats & Clark
Grey	318	8900
Lt. grey	3753	7031

Transfer - page 36, scroll transfer page 34

Monogram - grey satin stitch, 3 strands
Outline of monogram - grey back stitch, 2 strands
Scroll design - lt. grey satin stitch. 3 strands
Line under scroll design - stem stitch, 2 grey, 1 lt. grey strands
French knots - 2 strands

Make It Personal

Embroidery floss	DMC	Coats & Clark
Blue	926	6007
White		

Transfer - page 28

Stitch using 3 strands

Monogram - white satin stitch with blue laid work and cross bars over the satin stitch
Outlining - White back stitch

Hers

Embroidery floss	DMC	Coats & Clark
Pink	3326	3126

Transfer - page 30

Monogram - pink satin stitch, 3 strands

His

Embroidery floss	DMC	Coats & Clark
Blue	3844	7162

Transfer - page 30

Monogram - blue satin stitch, 3 strands

Dish Towels

Fiesta of Stitches #1

Embroidery floss	DMC	Coats & Clark
Yellow	743	2305
Orange	947	2330
Green	581	6256
Blue	995	7010
Purple	208	4301

Rows 1 and 5 - blue herringbone stitch, 3 strands
Row 2 - purple and orange laced running stitch, 3 strands
Row 3 - flowers - yellow lazy daisy, 3 strands
flower centers - orange French knots, 3 stran
vines - green stem stitch, 2 strands
leaves - green lazy daisy, 2 strands
Row 4 - purple scroll stitch, 3 strands

Pot Holders

Kitchen Stitches (vintage)

Embroidery floss	DMC	Coats & Clark
Blue	826	7022
Gold	742	2302
Red	321	3500
Black		

Transfer - page 30

Stitch using 3 strands

Creamer and sugar bowl - blue stem stitch
Hair - gold stem stitch
Eyes and brow - blue and black straight stitch and satin stitch
Pupils of eyes- black French knot
Mouth - red satin stitch
Nostrils - red straight stitch

Fiesta of Stitches #2

Embroidery floss	DMC	Coats & Clark
Blue	161	7150
Green	581	6256
Pink	600	3056
Yellow	743	2305

Stitch using 3 strands

Row 1 - green cross stitch
Row 2 - pink split stitch
Row 3 - flowers - yellow lazy daisy
flower centers - pink French knots
leaves - green lazy daisy
Row 4 - blue cross stitch

Table Runner

Very Vintage (vintage)

Embroidery floss	DMC	Coats & Clark
Gold	743	2295
Lt. Gold	744	2289
Green	988	6239
Blue	598	7976
Lt. Blue	828	7159
Pink	604	3087
Lt. Pink	605	3127
Ivory	712	2275
Black		

Transfer - page 20

Stitch using 2 strands

Rose centers - gold, pink and blue bullion knots
Roses - lt. gold, lt. pink and lt. blue bullion knots
Dot flowers - blue and lt. blue, pink and lt. pink, gold and lt. gold bullion knots and French knots
Small flowers - lt. gold, lt. pink, lt. blue French knots
Small flower centers - black French knots
Vines - green stem stitch
Leaves - green lazy daisy
Garland - blue and gold French knots
Scroll work - ivory stem stitch